The Usborne
Big Book
of
Holiday
Things to make and do

Fiona Watt & Rebecca Gilpin

Designed and illustrated by
Stella Baggott, Katrina Fearn, Non Figg, Erica Harrison,
Molly Sage and Josephine Thompson

Additional design by Amanda Barlow, Natacha Goransky, Michelle Lawrence,
Vici Leyhane, Katie Lovell, Sam Meredith, Antonia Miller and Rachel Wells.

Photographs by Howard Allman
Cover design by Amanda Gulliver

Contents

Pirate treasure map	4	Make a treasure chest	28
Parrot painting	6	Decorated eggs	30
Wax resist flowers	8	Tissue paper chains	32
Tractor picture	10	Collage fish	34
Mermaids to paint	12	Foil picture frame	36
Make an advent calendar	14	Mermaid mirror	38
Cut-and-stick mermaids	16	Make some beads	40
Pirate painting	18	Mermaid shell purse	42
Dolphins to draw	20	Carving pumpkins	44
Farmyard scene	22	Loveheart decoration	46
Handprinted mermaid	24	Make a mouse	48
Make some fairy wings	26	Sea horse pencil top	49

Pirate finger puppet	50	Mermaid tiara	74
Painted plant pot	52	Pirate paraphernalia	76
Octopus mobile	54	Printed collage card	78
Mermaid necklace	56	Zigzag Valentine card	80
Party masks	58	Easter egg card	82
Make a glitter bug	60	Painted butterflies card	84
Bouncing bats	62	Pop-up card	86
Party flags	64	Halloween card	88
Hanging fish chains	66	Snowman card	90
Pirate cutlass and hook	68	Reindeer wrapping paper	92
Cut-and-stick butterflies	70	Printed papers	94
Decorated boxes	72	Index	96

You'll find stickers in the middle of this book. You could use them to decorate the things you make.

Pirate treasure map

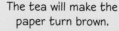
The tea will make the paper turn brown.

1. To make a piece of white paper look old, rip little strips from around its edges. Tightly crumple the paper, then open it out.

2. Pour some cold, strong tea into a dish. Then, lay the paper in the tea and push it down, so that the tea completely covers it.

3. Leave the paper to soak for about an hour. Then, lift it out and lay it on a piece of plastic foodwrap until it is dry.

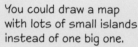
You could draw a map with lots of small islands instead of one big one.

4. Draw a big wiggly shape, for a treasure island. Then, draw a pirate ship and some waves near the top of the map.

5. Draw a flag and write 'TREASURE MAP' next to it. Add a compass in one corner, then draw some rocks around the island.

TREASURE MAP

Dead Man's Cave

Quicksand

Rugged Rascal Rocks

Misty Mountains

Shark-Infested Sea

Crocodile Swamp

Snake Forest

N

W   E

S

Look at the photo for different ideas.

6. Add waves and sharks' fins, for a shark-infested sea. Then, on the island, draw lots of dangers and write names next to them.

7. Fill in your picture with pencils. Then, mark where the treasure is hidden with a red 'X' and draw a dotted line from the ship to the X.

5

You could paint some
bright flowers on the tree.

Paint lots of green
leaves around the
parrot, too.

6

Parrot painting

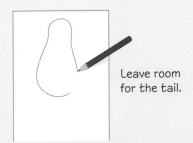

Leave room for the tail.

1. Draw a shape for the parrot's head and body, on a large piece of paper. Make the shape twice as long as your hand.

2. Draw an eye and a beak. Add some feathers on the side of the parrot's head. Then, draw a branch and two feet, like this.

Paint the feathers, too.

3. Using yellow paint, fill in the beak and the feet. Then, when the paint has dried, paint the body and the head with red paint.

Paint the tail over the branch.

4. Using long brushstrokes, paint a red tail. Let the paint dry, then add yellow feathers on top. Then, paint green feathers, too.

5. On an old plate, spread red, yellow, green and blue paint in stripes. Then, press your right hand into the paint, across all the stripes.

Print this wing first.

6. Turn the paper upside down. Then, using your hand, print a wing on the parrot. Make it overlap the parrot's body, like this.

7. Turn the plate around, so that the red paint is on the right-hand side. Then, print the parrot's other wing with your left hand.

8. Wash your hands, then paint a black dot on the eye. Leave the paint to dry. Then, paint the branch, using thick brown paint.

Wax resist flowers

Poppies

The shape has been drawn with an orange crayon here, so you can see it.

1. Draw a swirly shape with a white wax crayon or candle.

2. Brush paint on top of the waxy line to make a flower.

Daisies

1. Draw loopy petals, with the wax crayon or candle.

Paint green leaves around your flowers.

Tulips

2. Paint a flower like this, over the top of the petals.

1. Draw four upright petals with the crayon or candle.

2. Brush paint over the top of the lines you have drawn.

Draw, then paint a butterfly in the same way.

Tractor picture

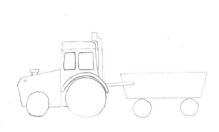

1. Draw two wheels with a pencil, making one bigger than the other. Then, draw the rest of the tractor. Add a trailer behind it.

2. Using wax crayons, draw over the outlines shown here. Add blue wavy lines on the window, then fill it in with a white crayon.

3. Draw lines and little round rivets on the tractor and trailer. Then, add hubcaps and V-shaped treads on the wheels.

4. Draw a row of big yellow spirals above the trailer, for hay bales. Then, add another row above them, and more rows above that.

The wax crayon will resist the paint.

5. Mix paints with water, to make them runny. Then, paint over each part of the picture and paint yellow ground at the bottom.

To add smoke, draw a swirl with a white wax crayon, then paint over it.

Draw stalks of corn around your tractor with an orange pencil.

6. When all the paint is completely dry, draw little mice between the hay bales with pencils. Add some stalks of corn, too.

11

Mermaids to paint

Leave some spaces between the lines.

1. Mix some watery blue paint. Then, scrunch up a kitchen paper towel and use it to paint wavy lines across a big piece of paper.

2. When the paint is dry, draw lots of curly waves with a blue pencil. Draw mermaids' heads above the waves and in the spaces.

3. Draw the hair, a neck and arms on each mermaid. Then, draw the body, stopping the lines where they meet a curly wave, like this.

Draw some curved lines on the ends of the tails.

4. Draw the end of a tail near each mermaid, poking out of the waves. Then, draw wavy patterns, for scales, on the bodies and the tails.

5. Draw the mermaids' faces. Then, roughly fill in the bodies and tails with purple, green and blue pencils. Fill in their hair, too.

6. Draw little fish in the gaps between the mermaids, then fill them in. Add some splashes of water around the fish and the mermaids.

7. Mix some white paint with a little water on an old plate or saucer. Dip a paintbrush into the paint, then hold it above the paper.

8. Flick your finger across the bristles of the brush so that the paint splatters onto the paper. Splatter more paint again and again.

Make an advent calendar

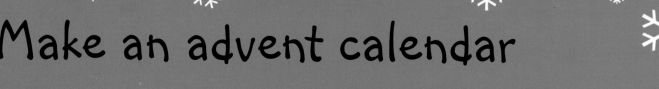

1. Cut a piece of bright cardboard or thick paper the same size as this book, when it's opened out.

2. For the tree, fold a large rectangle of green paper in half, so that the long sides are together.

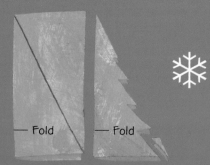

— Fold   — Fold

3. Draw a diagonal line with a ruler, then cut along it. Cut out small triangles along the open edge.

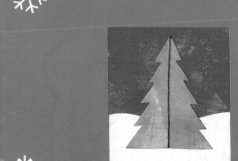

4. Cut a white shape for the snow. Glue it on. Then, open out the tree and glue it in the middle.

You will need 24 altogether.

5. For the 'doors', draw different shapes. You could also use stickers from the sticker pages.

Glue down here only.

6. Cut out all the shapes you have drawn. Put glue along one edge of each shape and press it on.

Make sure your picture is smaller than the door.

7. Draw a small Christmas picture behind each door, or press on a sticker from the sticker pages.

8. Decorate the tree around the doors with extra stickers and shapes cut from paper.

9. Use a felt-tip pen to write a number on each door. Start at one and go up to 24.

As you open each door during December, fold it back, so that it stays open.

Cut-and-stick mermaid

1. Cut a small rectangle of book covering film. Draw a shape for a mermaid's tail on the backing paper and cut it out.

2. Sprinkle glitter onto a plate. Peel most of the backing paper from the end of the tail, then dip the sticky side in the glitter.

Fold the tail back from here.

The seaweed and fish in this picture were cut from paper and decorated with glitter.

3. Peel off all the backing paper and press the sticky end onto some paper. Fold the tail back, so that the glitter is at the front.

4. Mix paint for the skin on an old plate. Cut a small rectangle of thick cardboard and dip one long edge into the paint.

16

Twist this end a little as you drag it.

For a curved arm like the one above, bend the cardboard as you print it.

5. Place the edge of the cardboard next to the tail. Then, drag it a little way across the paper for the mermaid's body.

6. Dip the edge of the cardboard in the paint again and print two lines for her arms. Fingerprint a circle for her head.

You'll need to dip your finger in the paint a few times.

Shake off any excess glitter.

7. When the paint is dry, spread some yellow paint onto the plate. Dip your little finger into the paint and fingerprint some hair.

8. Use a felt-tip pen to add a face. Then, brush a band of white glue for a bikini top and sprinkle glitter over it. Leave it to dry.

Pirate painting

The wax resists the paint.

The salt makes a watery effect.

1. Using a white or pale blue wax crayon, draw lots of curling waves across the bottom of a long sheet of white paper.

2. Mix some blue paint with water, to make it watery. Paint over the top line of the waves, then fill in the area below the line.

3. Brush more paint over the wet paint. Then, while it is still wet, sprinkle salt over it. Leave the paint to dry completely.

You could add a shark's fin or a floating barrel to another row of waves.

 Use a pencil.

4. When the paint is dry, brush off any excess salt. Then, draw a pirate ship, with masts and sails, near one end of the painting.

5. At the other end of the paper from the ship, draw a circle for a pirate's head. Add a headscarf and a face, then draw the arms.

6. Paint the ship and the pirate, then leave them to dry. When they are dry, go over the lines with a thin black felt-tip pen.

This big picture was made by cutting out two rows of waves and gluing them together.

Dolphins to draw

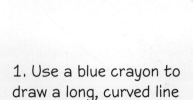

1. Use a blue crayon to draw a long, curved line for the tummy.

2. Draw another curved line above the first one for the dolphin's back.

3. Add a long curved shape at the top. This is the dolphin's nose.

4. Add a fin on the top of the body and one underneath, like this.

5. Draw an eye and add a line inside the nose, for a mouth.

6. Add a tail, then fill in all the shapes with a blue felt-tip pen.

A fish

Fill in the tail and fins with a pen.

1. Draw the body with a red or orange crayon. Add an eye and a mouth.

2. Crayon some patterns on the body. Fill in with a felt-tip pen.

3. Add a tail and two fins with a crayon. Add some air bubbles near its mouth.

20

You could use this idea
to decorate invitations
for a swimming party.

Farmyard scene

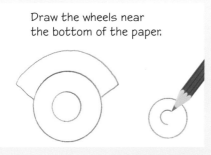

Draw the wheels near the bottom of the paper.

1. Pressing lightly, draw a tractor wheel on a big piece of white paper. Add a hubcap and a mudguard. Then, draw a smaller wheel, too.

2. Starting at the top of the mudguard, draw a shape for the front of the tractor. Add a pipe, then draw a grill on the side and one at the front.

3. Draw a farmer sitting on the mudguard, holding a steering wheel. Draw his head, but don't draw his eye and mouth yet.

4. For chickens, draw small half circles. Add feathers at one end of each half circle, for their tails. Then, draw more feathers for wings.

Look at the big picture for other ideas.

5. Draw a barn above the tractor. Then, add a roof, doors with a lock and a window. Add a hedge and other animals.

6. Draw over all the pencil outlines with felt-tip pens. Then, add curved treads on the wheels and bolts on the hubcaps.

Rinse the brush after painting each part of the picture.

7. To fill in the tractor, dip a clean paintbrush into water. Brush in from the outlines, to spread the ink. Then, fill in the rest of the picture.

Draw eyes, beaks and combs on the chickens.

8. Leave the ink to dry. Then, draw the farmer's face with thin pens. Draw details on the chickens and other animals, too.

9. For the background, fill in all the white spaces with watery brown paint. Leave a white border around each part of the picture, like this.

Try adding a painted sun and sky.

You could add the farmer's wife on another tractor.

Draw curved lines for smoke.

Handprinted mermaid

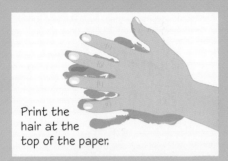

Print the hair at the top of the paper.

1. Spread paint for the hair on a plate. Press your hand in the paint and press it on some paper. Do another print on top.

2. When the paint is dry, mix some paint for the skin. Fingerpaint around and around for a head, on top of the hair.

Drag your finger across the paper.

3. Fingerpaint the top of her body. Then, dip your finger in the paint again and paint two arms. Leave the paint to dry.

Keep your fingers together when you print it.

4. Turn the paper around. Press your hand in blue paint and do a handprint for the tail. The tail should overlap the body.

5. Press your three middle fingers into the paint and print them at the bottom of the tail. Then, make another print, like this.

6. When the paint is dry, fingerprint dots of bright blue paint onto the tail for scales. Print a row of green scales at the top, too.

7. Press your finger into some white paint and print two eyes. Let them dry, then use your little finger to dot blue on top.

8. Print small blue dots in the eyes and a pink dot for lips. When the paint is dry, use felt-tip pens to draw eyelashes and a mouth.

Fingerprint patterns onto the body, too.

9. Add some fish by fingerpainting around and around for the body. Then, fingerprint two dots for the tail.

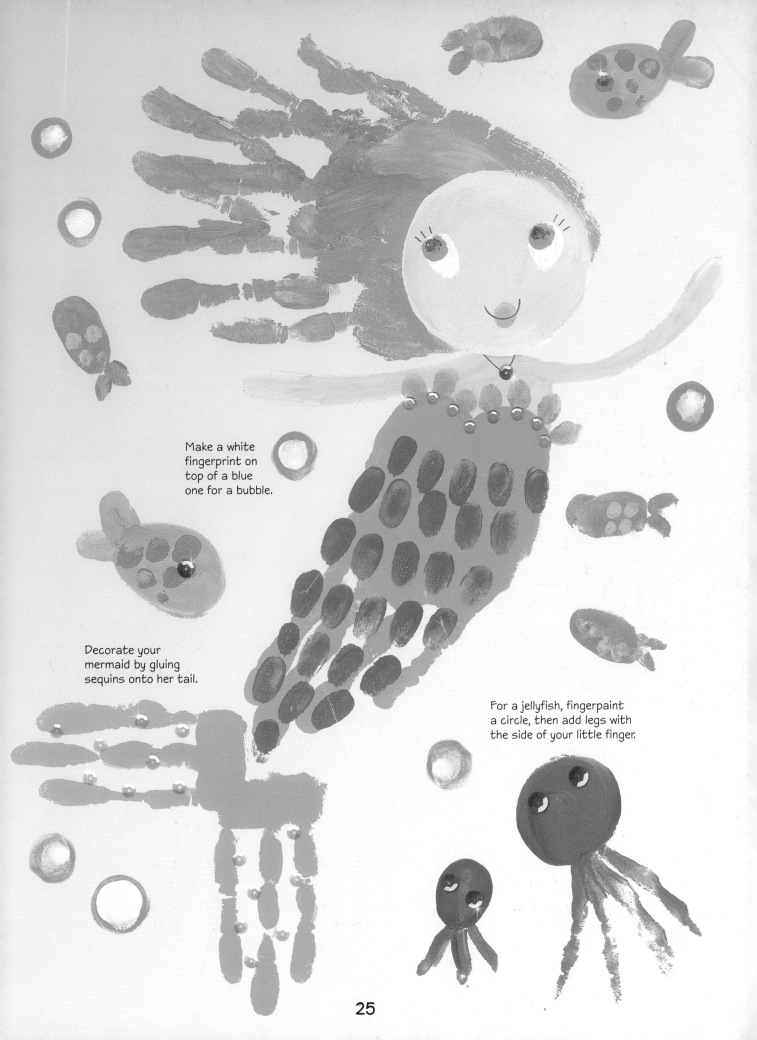

Make a white
fingerprint on
top of a blue
one for a bubble.

Decorate your
mermaid by gluing
sequins onto her tail.

For a jellyfish, fingerpaint
a circle, then add legs with
the side of your little finger.

Make some fairy wings

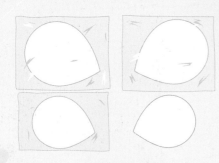

1. Draw two big wing shapes and two smaller ones on paper. Then, cut them out and lay plastic foodwrap over them.

2. Rip up two shades of tissue paper and overlap the pieces on the plastic. Cover the wing shapes, including their edges.

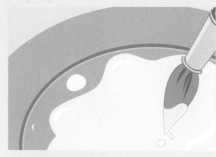

3. Mix some white glue with water so that it is runny. Then, use a thick paintbrush to paint glue all over the pieces of tissue paper.

4. Press on another layer of tissue paper and paint it with glue. Then, add about five more layers of tissue paper and glue.

Put the wings on your back and ask someone to tie the ribbons at the front.

Press on shiny stickers to make the wings even more sparkly.

5. Sprinkle the top layer of glue with glitter. When it is dry, paint another layer of glue over the glitter. Leave the glue to dry.

6. Peel the wings off the foodwrap. Lay the paper wings on top, then draw around them and cut out the shapes.

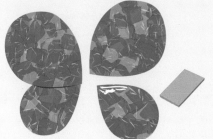

7. Glue the wings together, like this. Then, while the glue is drying, cut a rectangle from some thick cardboard.

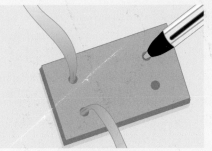

8. Using a ballpoint pen, carefully make four holes in the rectangle. Then, thread two long pieces of ribbon through the holes.

Leave long ends on the ribbons.

9. Glue the rectangle onto the back of the wings, with the ends of the ribbons sticking out. Then, let the glue dry.

Make a treasure chest

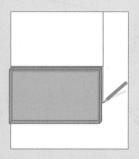

1. For the top of the chest, lay the lid of a shoe box on a large piece of thin cardboard. Then, draw around it twice, like this.

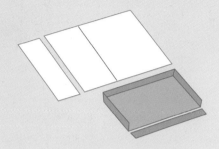

2. Cut around the shape, then cut a strip off one end. Then, cut one of the long sides off the lid of the shoe box.

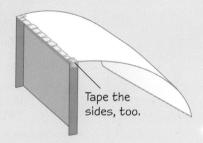

Tape the sides, too.

3. Tape one of the short edges of the cardboard along the remaining long side of the lid, using lots of small pieces of sticky tape.

Crease the fold well.

4. Fold up the edge of the cardboard that hasn't been taped. The folded part will be glued onto the box, to make the chest's hinge.

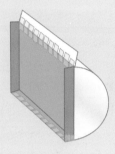

5. To make the top curve, tape the folded edge of the hinge to the lid, like this. Secure it with lots of small pieces of tape.

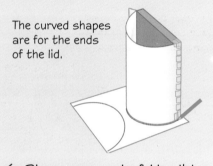

The curved shapes are for the ends of the lid.

6. Place one end of the lid at the edge of a piece of cardboard. Draw around the curve, then move the lid. Draw around it again.

Don't tape the hinge.

7. Cut out the curved shapes. Then, tape one shape onto each end of the lid, matching the edges as well as you can.

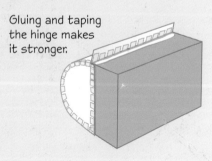

Gluing and taping the hinge makes it stronger.

8. Put the lid on the chest. Spread white glue along the edge of the chest, then press down the hinge and tape it, to secure it.

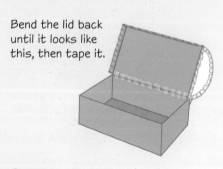

Bend the lid back until it looks like this, then tape it.

9. When the glue is dry, gently open the lid of the chest. Then, tape all the way along the hinge, inside the chest.

Put the chest on
a newspaper.

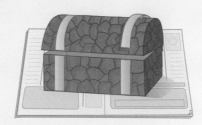
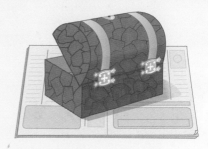

10. Rip lots of tissue paper
into large pieces. Brush
glue onto the chest and
press on pieces of tissue
paper, until it is covered.

11. For straps, cut two
strips of paper, and glue
them onto the front of
the chest. Then, glue two
longer strips onto the lid.

12. Press the lock and
hinges from the sticker
pages onto the front and
back of the chest, or draw
your own and glue them on.

Fill your treasure chest
with coins, jewels and
other shiny treasure.

Decorated eggs

You don't need the yolk and egg white.

1. Tap an egg sharply on the rim of a mug to make a crack. Then, use your fingers to carefully break the egg in half over the mug.

2. Wash the eggshells carefully and leave them to dry. Then, hold one half and brush white glue along its cracked edge.

Match the cracked edges if you can.

3. Carefully fit the other half on top. Brush more glue around the crack to seal it. Put it in an egg carton to dry.

4. Rip a piece of tissue paper into lots of small pieces. Then, brush the top half of the egg with white glue.

5. Press pieces of tissue paper onto the wet glue. Brush on more glue and tissue paper, until the top half is covered.

6. Leave the glue to dry. Then, hold the top half and cover the bottom half with tissue paper in the same way. Leave it to dry.

Decorate one side first, then let it dry.

7. Mix some bright paint with a little white glue on an old plate. Paint one half of the egg and leave it to dry. Then, paint the rest.

8. When the paint is dry, mix other shades of paint. Use a thin paintbrush to decorate your egg with flowers and spots.

Make up patterns of your own or use the ideas shown here.

Tissue paper chains

Tape the flowers onto a window, so that the light shines through them.

1. Lay a large piece of plastic foodwrap on an old magazine. Then, rip two shades of pink tissue paper into lots of pieces.

2. Lay pieces of tissue paper on the foodwrap, overlapping each other. Cover as much of the foodwrap as you can.

3. Mix some white glue with water so that it is runny. Then, paint glue over the pieces of tissue paper, until they are covered.

4. Add another layer of tissue paper and glue. Then, add a third layer of paper and glue, and sprinkle glitter on the top.

5. When the glue is dry, paint glue over the glitter and let it dry. Then, lay another piece of foodwrap on a newspaper.

6. Make layers of orange and yellow tissue paper and glue, as you did before. Add glitter and glue and leave it to dry.

You could make lots of chains and hang them up.

You could put sparkly flowers into a card so that they tumble out when it's opened.

7. Peel the glittery tissue paper off the foodwrap. Then, cut out pink flowers and small pink circles. Cut out some orange ones too.

8. Glue the orange circles onto the middle of the pink flowers. Glue pink circles onto the middle of the orange flowers.

9. Then, cut some thin ribbon into pieces which are different lengths and tape the flowers onto the ribbons, to make a chain.

Collage fish

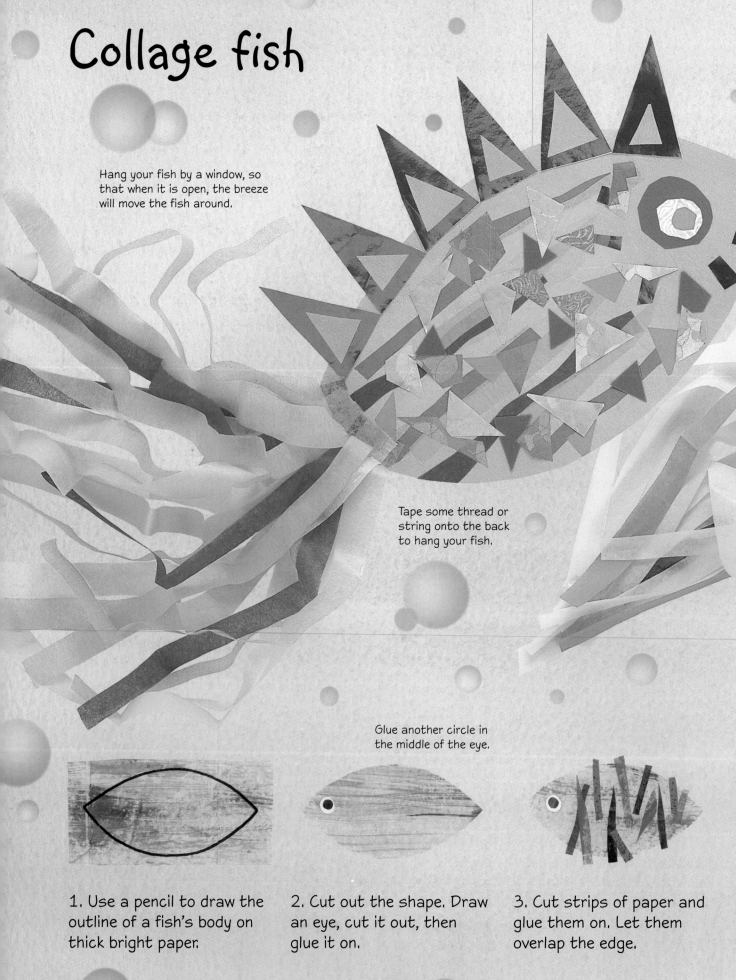

Hang your fish by a window, so that when it is open, the breeze will move the fish around.

Tape some thread or string onto the back to hang your fish.

Glue another circle in the middle of the eye.

1. Use a pencil to draw the outline of a fish's body on thick bright paper.

2. Cut out the shape. Draw an eye, cut it out, then glue it on.

3. Cut strips of paper and glue them on. Let them overlap the edge.

Use different types of paper, such as shiny paper and tissue paper, to decorate your fish.

4. Glue shapes on top of the strips. Trim off any pieces which overlap the edge.

5. Cut some triangles of paper. Glue them along the top of the body.

6. Cut long strips of bright tissue paper. Glue them on to make a tail.

Foil picture frame

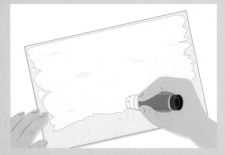

1. Cut a large piece of kitchen foil. Using a glue stick, spread glue all over the non-shiny side, then fold the foil in half.

2. Rub the foil so that the two layers stick together and the surface is smooth. Then, put the folded foil onto an old magazine.

3. Pressing hard with a ballpoint pen, draw a rectangle on the foil, then draw a smaller rectangle inside it, like this.

4. Draw lots of flowers between the lines. Then, cut around the rectangles with scissors, a little way from the outside line.

5. Push a ballpoint pen through the foil, to make a hole for your scissors. Then, cut all the way around the inside line, to make a frame.

Don't worry if the edges aren't straight.

6. Lay the foil frame onto some thin cardboard and draw a bigger rectangle around it, like this. Then, cut out the shape.

7. Lay the foil frame onto the cardboard again and draw around the hole. Push a pen through the shape you've drawn.

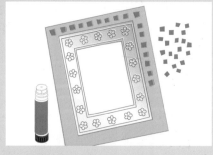

8. Cut out the shape, then glue the foil frame onto the cardboard one. Cut out lots of paper squares and glue them onto the frame.

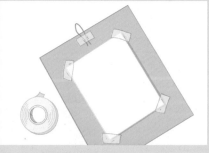

9. Lay the frame on a picture, then turn them both over and tape the picture in place. Tape a loop of string at the top.

You could draw flowers and leaves on foil and cut them out separately.

You could make a picture of yourself from paper to go in the frame.

You could just put a photo of you in the frame, of course!

37

Mermaid mirror

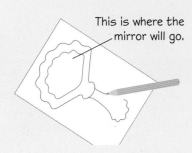

This is where the mirror will go.

1. Draw a big shell for the frame on the top half of a piece of cardboard. Then, draw a smaller shell inside it and add a handle.

2. Cut out the frame. To make the back of the mirror, draw around the frame on another piece of cardboard and cut it out.

You don't need these pieces.

3. To cut out the smaller shell, cut straight across the frame, like this. Then, cut out the small shell from both pieces.

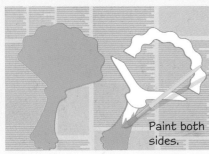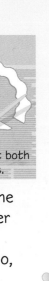

Paint both sides.

4. Put the frame and the back on some newspaper and paint them. Paint around all the edges too, then leave them to dry.

Start here

5. Tape the frame together, and lay it on the non-shiny side of some kitchen foil. Then, draw around the top of the frame.

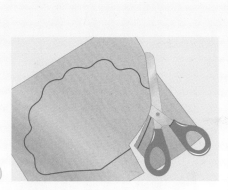

6. Draw a line across the bottom of the shape. Then, cut out a shape for the mirror a little way inside the outline.

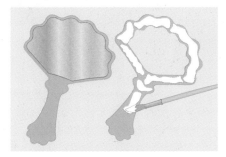

7. Glue the foil onto the back with the shiny side facing up. Spread glue on the frame and press it on top. Leave it to dry.

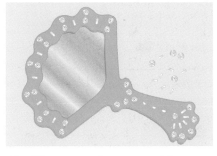

8. Glue sequins over the joins in the frame to hide them. Then, decorate the frame with more sequins and some beads.

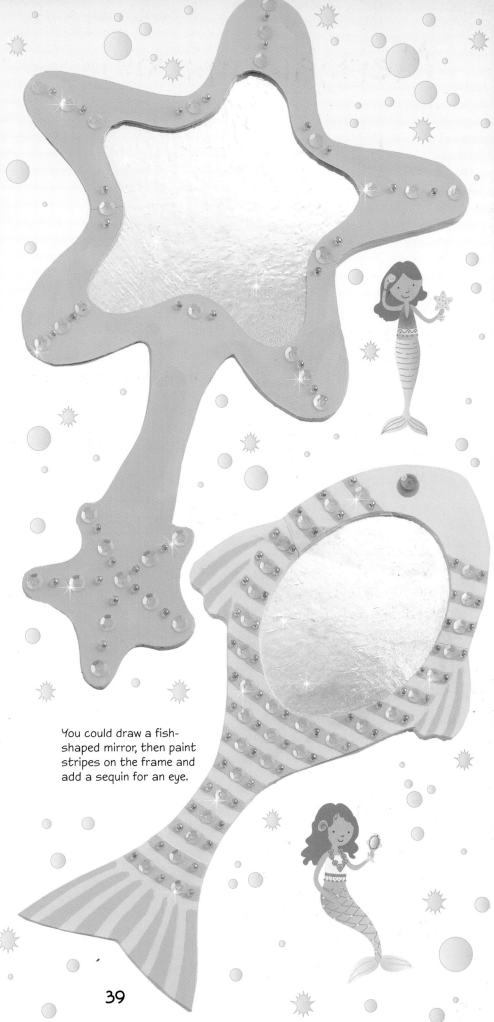

You could draw a fish-shaped mirror, then paint stripes on the frame and add a sequin for an eye.

Make some beads

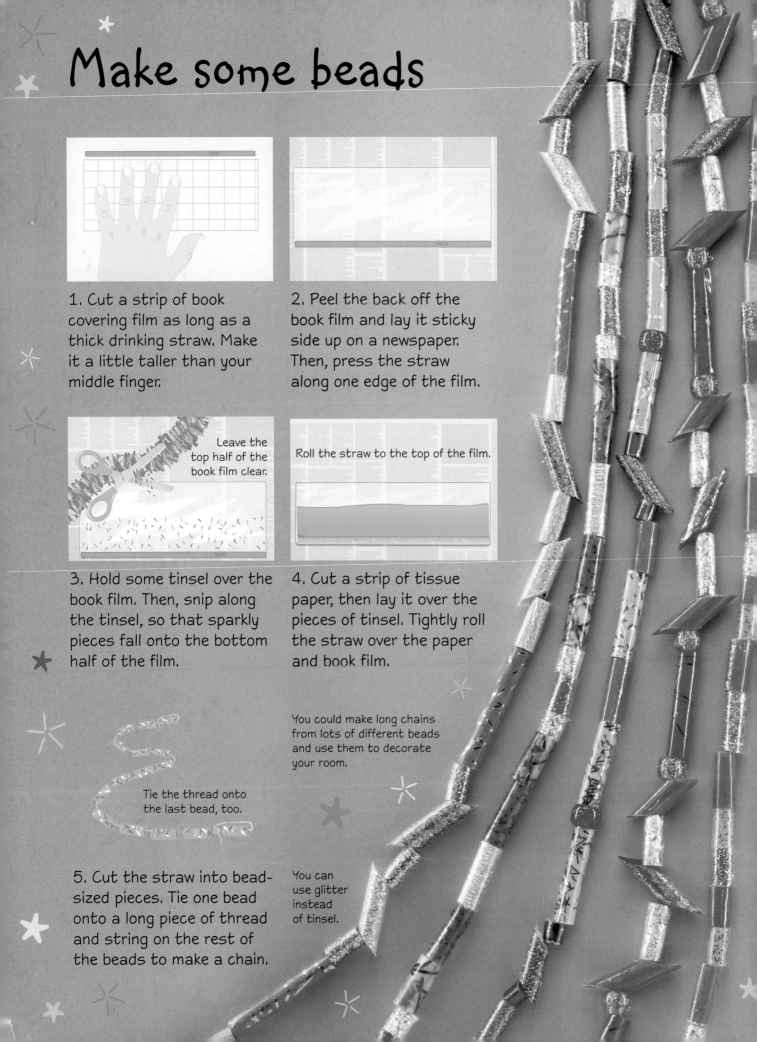

1. Cut a strip of book covering film as long as a thick drinking straw. Make it a little taller than your middle finger.

2. Peel the back off the book film and lay it sticky side up on a newspaper. Then, press the straw along one edge of the film.

Leave the top half of the book film clear.

Roll the straw to the top of the film.

3. Hold some tinsel over the book film. Then, snip along the tinsel, so that sparkly pieces fall onto the bottom half of the film.

4. Cut a strip of tissue paper, then lay it over the pieces of tinsel. Tightly roll the straw over the paper and book film.

You could make long chains from lots of different beads and use them to decorate your room.

Tie the thread onto the last bead, too.

5. Cut the straw into bead-sized pieces. Tie one bead onto a long piece of thread and string on the rest of the beads to make a chain.

You can use glitter instead of tinsel.

More ideas

Instead of sparkly beads, try making shiny ones. Place a strip of kitchen foil next to a straw and roll the straw up.

Leave a large part of the foodwrap clear, so that it clings onto the straw.

Lay a straw along a large piece of plastic foodwrap and roll it twice. Snip pieces of tissue paper over the foodwrap, then roll it up.

These beads were cut at an angle.

Lay the ribbon shiny side down.

To make striped beads, cut pieces of gift ribbon and lay them on the book film, like this. Lay the straw on one edge and roll it up.

The bead below was made using plastic foodwrap.

You could thread ordinary beads on, too.

41

Make a jewel for fastening by following steps 6-7 on page 57.

Mermaid shell purse

Make the teardrop a little longer than your middle finger.

1. Draw a teardrop shape with long, straight sides on thick paper. Cut it out and draw around it four times. Cut out the shapes.

2. Hold one teardrop like this. Then, push the sides together to make it curved. Make all the teardrops curved in this way.

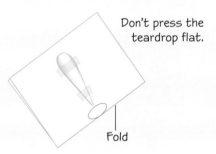

Don't press the teardrop flat.

Fold

3. Fold a large piece of thin cardboard in half and draw an oval on the fold. Tape one of the teardrops above the oval, like this.

4. Tape on the rest of the teardrops and draw a shell shape around them. Then, keeping the cardboard folded, cut out the shell.

Fold over any tissue paper that overlaps the edges.

5. Rip lots of small pieces of tissue paper. Brush white glue over the shell and press on the paper, but don't squash the teardrops.

Put the strip to one side for step 8.

6. Lay the shell on a piece of paper. Draw around it and cut out the shape. Then, cut a strip of paper as long as the paper shell.

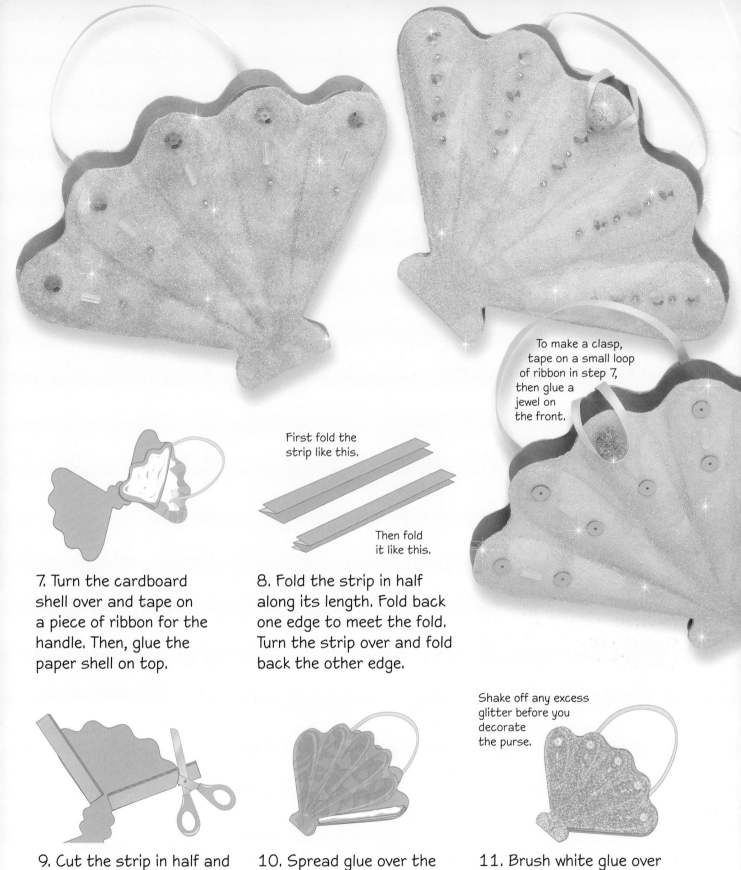

To make a clasp, tape on a small loop of ribbon in step 7, then glue a jewel on the front.

First fold the strip like this.

Then fold it like this.

7. Turn the cardboard shell over and tape on a piece of ribbon for the handle. Then, glue the paper shell on top.

8. Fold the strip in half along its length. Fold back one edge to meet the fold. Turn the strip over and fold back the other edge.

Shake off any excess glitter before you decorate the purse.

9. Cut the strip in half and glue the pieces in a V-shape on one half of the shell. Trim the ends of the strips to fit the shell.

10. Spread glue over the top layer of the folded strips. Then, fold the other side of the purse on top of the strips.

11. Brush white glue over the bumpy side of the purse and sprinkle glitter over it. Decorate the purse with sequins and beads.

Carving pumpkins

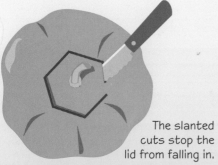
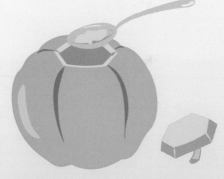
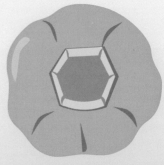

The slanted cuts stop the lid from falling in.

1. Get someone to help you make six slanted cuts in the top of the pumpkin, for a lid. Make the cuts join each other.

2. Then, use a spoon or an ice-cream scoop to clean out all the seeds and the stringy pieces inside the pumpkin.

3. Scrape away the wall of the pumpkin gradually, until it is about 3cm (1in.) thick. You may need some help with this.

Draw big shapes for the face. They are easier to cut out and let the candle light shine through.

Use a knife with a serrated edge.

4. Use a felt-tip pen to draw eyes, a nose and a mouth on the pumpkin. Don't make them too small or close together.

5. Use a small knife to cut around the eyes. Push the cut pieces inside the pumpkin, then shake them out of the top.

6. Cut around the nose and push it in. Then, cut around the mouth in sections. Don't try to cut it all in one piece.

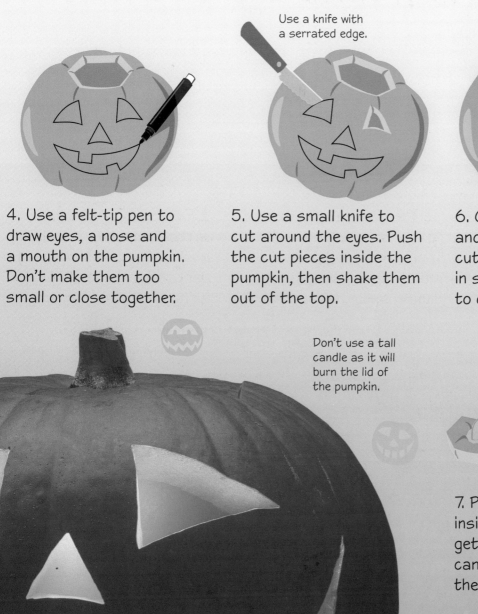

Don't use a tall candle as it will burn the lid of the pumpkin.

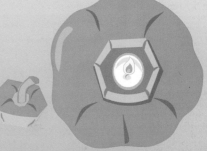

7. Put a small candle inside the pumpkin. Then, get someone to light the candle for you and put the lid on top.

Carve your pumpkin only two or three days before Halloween, as it will begin to soften.

Loveheart decoration

For a pretty decoration, glue several lovehearts onto a long ribbon.

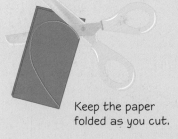

Keep the paper folded as you cut.

1. Fold a small piece of pink paper in half. Then, draw half a heart against the fold. Cut out the shape, then open out the heart.

2. Cut a rectangle that is about the size of a postcard from thick pink paper. Then, lay a pencil along one of the long edges.

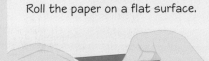

Roll the paper on a flat surface.

3. Curl the paper tightly around the pencil. Then, roll the pencil up the paper to the top edge. Unroll it and remove the pencil.

4. Fold in the edge that was curled around the pencil, to make it easier to roll. Then, roll the paper again, as tightly as you can.

The slices get flattened by the scissors.

5. Cut the rolled paper into lots of slices. Then, to make the slices more like round roses, gently squash them a little.

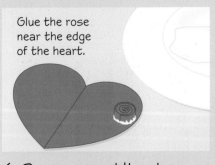

Glue the rose near the edge of the heart.

6. Pour some white glue onto an old plate. Dip the bottom of a rose into the glue and press the rose onto the heart.

The lovehearts look pretty glued onto a card, too.

You could glue a loveheart onto a little gift box.

If you need a few more roses, make another roll of paper.

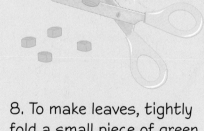

7. Glue another rose next to the first one. Glue more roses around the edge of the heart, then glue the rest in the middle.

8. To make leaves, tightly fold a small piece of green paper, along its long edge, several times. Then, cut the folded paper into slices.

9. Dip a leaf into the glue and press it into a gap between two roses. Glue on lots more leaves, then leave the glue to dry.

Make a mouse

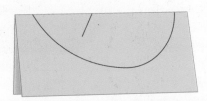

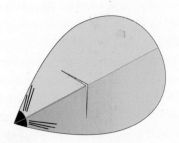

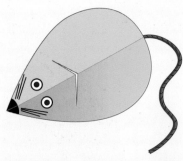

1. For a mouse's body, fold a piece of thick paper in half. Draw a curve against the fold and a short line down from the fold, like this.

2. Keeping the paper folded, cut along the curve and the short line. Then, flatten the body and draw a nose and whiskers.

3. Draw two eyes on white paper, then cut them out. Glue them onto the body. Then, for a tail, cut a piece of string and tape it on.

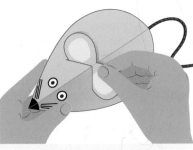

4. Fold another piece of paper in half, for the ears. Draw an ear against the fold, then cut along the line. Open out the ears.

5. Cut two shapes from pink paper and glue them onto the ears. Then, slot the ears into the cut at the top of the body.

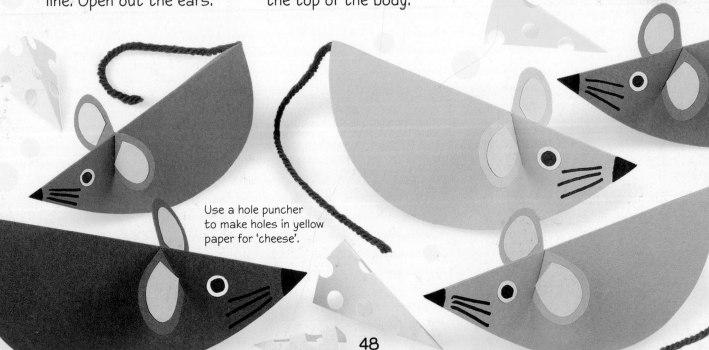

Use a hole puncher to make holes in yellow paper for 'cheese'.

48

Sea horse pencil top

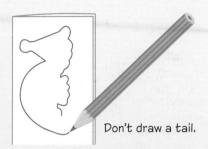

Don't draw a tail.

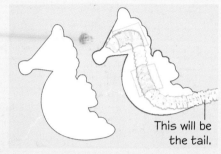

This will be the tail.

1. Fold a piece of thick paper in half. Draw a sea horse's body, then cut out the shape through both layers of paper.

2. Bend a pipe cleaner into a curved shape which follows the sea horse's body, like this. Then, tape the pipe cleaner in place.

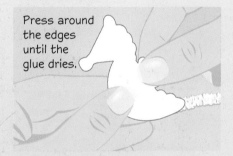

Press around the edges until the glue dries.

3. Spread white glue over the paper and the pipe cleaner. Then, press the other sea horse on top and squeeze the edges together.

4. When the glue is dry, paint both sides of the sea horse's body and all along its edges. Paint the pipe cleaner, too.

5. When the paint is dry, paint patterns and eyes on both sides of the sea horse. Then, wind the tail around the end of a pencil.

You could make a sea horse to give as a present.

Make a sea horse charm like this one by curling the tail into a spiral.

Pirate finger puppet

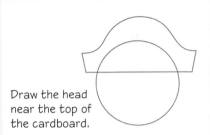

Draw the head near the top of the cardboard.

1. For the pirate's head, draw a circle on a piece of thin cardboard. Draw a line across the circle, then draw a hat above the line.

2. Add a scarf below the hat, then draw ears and a face. Draw a body and two arms. Then, add two lines down the body.

3. Draw a pair of shorts on black paper and cut them out. Lay them below the body and draw around them. Then, lift them off.

Cut a little way away from the pirate.

4. Draw a circle on each leg. Use felt-tip pens to draw over all the lines and fill in the clothes. Then, cut around the pirate.

The holes are for your fingers.

5. Cut up into the circles, then cut around them. Spread glue along the top of the shorts and press them onto his legs.

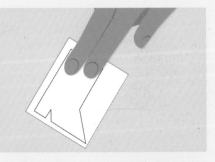

6. For the pirate's boots, draw a boot on thick paper, making the leg part as wide as two fingers, like this. Then, cut it out.

Push your fingers through the holes, then push on the boots and wiggle your fingers.

The tab is used when you glue the boots together.

7. Fold a piece of paper in half and lay the boot on it. Draw around the boot, then turn it over and draw around it again, like this.

8. Draw a tab on the side of one of the boot outlines. Then, holding the layers together, cut around the shape, including the tab.

9. Fold one of the boots in half, then fold the tab inside the boot, glue it and press hard. Make the other boot in the same way.

Painted plant pot

Spotted pot

1. Wash a terracotta flower pot thoroughly with water, to remove any soil. Then, leave the pot to dry out completely overnight.

Paint inside the top, too.

2. Paint the outside of the pot with white acrylic paint. Leave the paint to dry, then paint some light purple circles on the pot.

Make the circles different sizes.

3. Paint darker purple and yellow circles in the spaces. Then, paint more circles on top and leave the paint to dry.

You could put a plant in the pot, and give it to someone as a present.

You could press on stickers from the middle of this book.

The spots on the pot above were fingerpainted.

Flowery pot

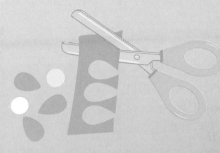

1. Wash a flower pot, let it dry, then paint it pale pink. Cut some circles and petal shapes from different shades of thin paper.

Use a glue stick.

2. Glue some of the petals onto the pot to make a flower. Then, glue a circle in the middle of the flower and add another flower.

The glue is clear when it dries.

3. Paint a thick layer of white glue all over the outside of the pot, including the flowers. Leave the glue to dry.

You could decorate a base, too.

This mobile had an extra thread taped to the middle of the octopus' body after it was slotted together.

54

Octopus mobile

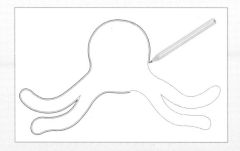

1. Draw an octopus with four legs on some cardboard. Cut it out, then draw around it on another piece of cardboard.

The slit should reach just over halfway.

2. Cut out the second octopus. Then, hold the bodies together, with one upside down. Cut a slit into both of the bodies.

3. Lay both bodies on some newspaper. Then, paint both sides of them with orange paint. Leave them to dry.

4. Dip a dry paintbrush into blue paint. Then, flick your finger across the bristles to splatter lots of paint over the bodies.

5. On another piece of cardboard, draw lots of different fish to hang from the mobile. Then, cut out all the shapes.

You could tape more than one fish onto a thread.

6. Cut eight different lengths of thread. Then, tape the fish onto the thread with small pieces of sticky tape.

Paint over the tape, too.

7. Lay the fish on clean newspaper. Decorate both sides with bright paints and let the paint dry. Then, add faces with a felt-tip pen.

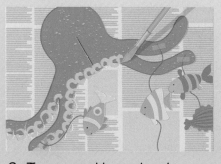

8. Tape one thread onto each leg of the octopus. Then, paint blue rings along the bottom edge of each leg for the suckers.

9. Let the paint dry. Then, slot the slit of one body into the other slit. Draw a face and open the mobile. Add a thread for hanging.

Mermaid necklace

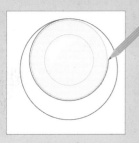

1. Draw around a small plate on thin white cardboard. Then, lay a saucer at the top of the circle and draw around it.

2. Rip some pink tissue paper into small pieces. Brush white glue on the part between the circles and press on the paper.

3. When the glue is dry, draw wavy lines along the edges of the two circles, like this. Then, cut out the necklace along these lines.

4. Turn the necklace over. Draw a line around the middle of the necklace with a ballpoint pen. Press hard as you draw.

You could use sequins to decorate your necklace, too.

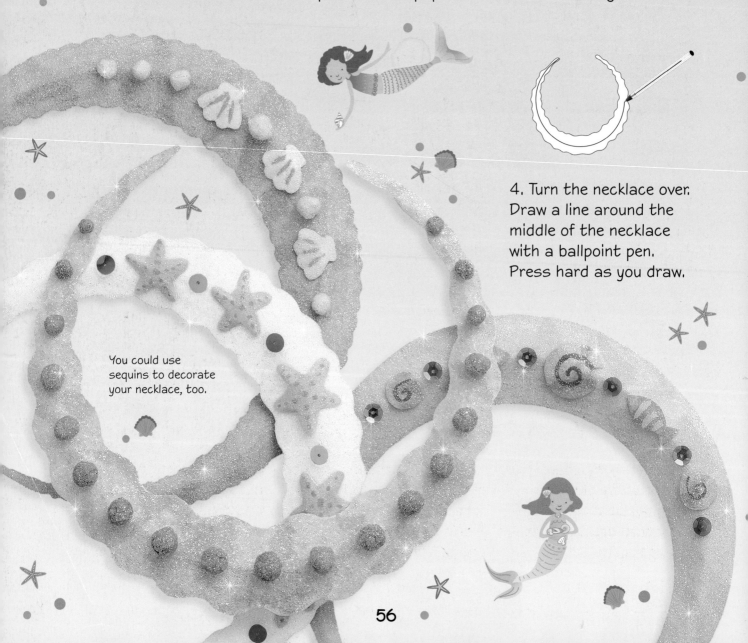

56

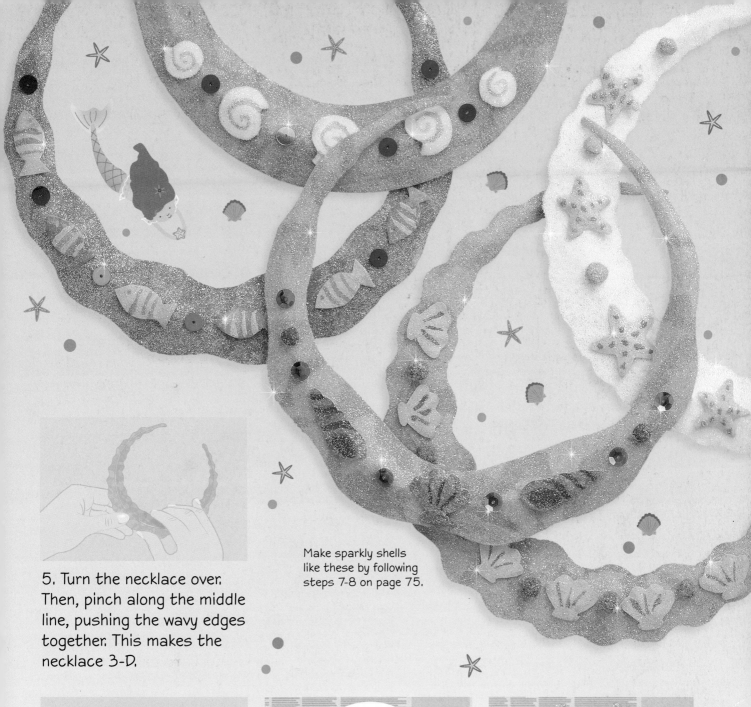

Make sparkly shells like these by following steps 7-8 on page 75.

5. Turn the necklace over. Then, pinch along the middle line, pushing the wavy edges together. This makes the necklace 3-D.

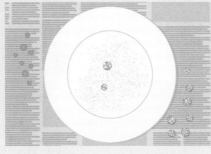

6. For a jewel, dip your fingers in white glue and roll a small piece of tissue paper into a ball between your fingers.

7. Sprinkle glitter onto an old plate and roll the jewel in the glitter. Make lots of jewels of different sizes in the same way.

Glue the small jewels near the ends.

8. Brush white glue over the necklace and lightly sprinkle on some glitter. Then, glue on the jewels to decorate the necklace.

Party masks

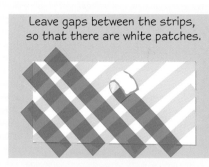

Leave gaps between the strips, so that there are white patches.

1. Cut a piece of pink and a piece of blue tissue paper into long strips. The strips should be the width of two of your fingers.

2. Glue the blue strips diagonally across a piece of cardboard, leaving gaps between them. Then, glue the pink strips over them.

3. When the glue is dry, turn the cardboard over. Lay a pair of sunglasses on the cardboard, like this, and draw around them.

Use the outline of the sunglasses as a guide for the eyeholes.

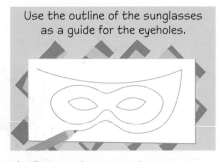

4. Draw shapes where your eyes will be. Then, draw a mask around the outline of the glasses. Cut out the mask you have drawn.

5. Press the point of a sharp pencil through the eyeholes. Push one scissor blade into the holes. Then, cut out both eyeholes.

6. Turn the mask over. Draw lines of glitter glue along all the edges of the tissue paper strips. Let the glitter glue dry.

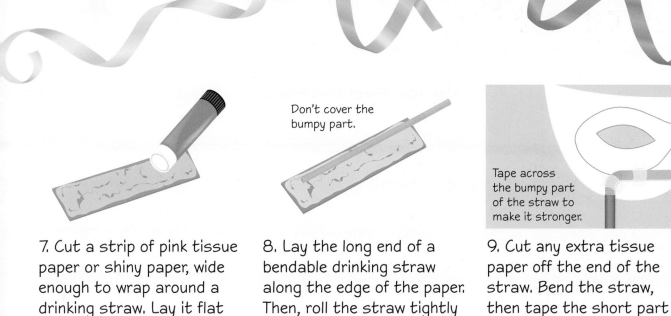

Don't cover the bumpy part.

Tape across the bumpy part of the straw to make it stronger.

7. Cut a strip of pink tissue paper or shiny paper, wide enough to wrap around a drinking straw. Lay it flat and cover it with glue.

8. Lay the long end of a bendable drinking straw along the edge of the paper. Then, roll the straw tightly in the paper.

9. Cut any extra tissue paper off the end of the straw. Bend the straw, then tape the short part to the back of your mask.

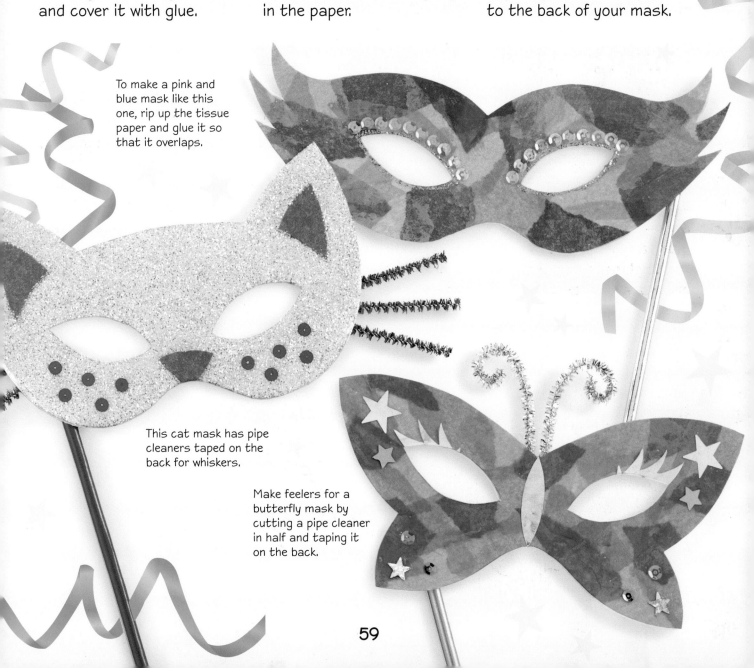

To make a pink and blue mask like this one, rip up the tissue paper and glue it so that it overlaps.

This cat mask has pipe cleaners taped on the back for whiskers.

Make feelers for a butterfly mask by cutting a pipe cleaner in half and taping it on the back.

Make a glitter bug

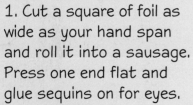

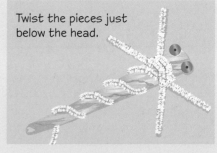

Don't cut this end off.

Twist the pieces just below the head.

1. Cut a square of foil as wide as your hand span and roll it into a sausage. Press one end flat and glue sequins on for eyes.

2. Wind a pipe cleaner along the length of the body from just below the eyes. Leave any extra as you will need it later.

3. For the wings, cut a pipe cleaner in half. Twist one half around the body. Twist on the other half too, then bend the ends out, like this.

4. To print the wings, place a leaf, with the veins facing up, on some newspaper. Lightly brush over the leaf with silver or gold paint.

5. Press the painted side of the leaf onto some tissue paper to print four leaves. Cut them out when the paint is dry.

Most of these bugs were made with shiny craft foil.

6. Lay the wings painted side down. Put the bug on top, upside down, like this. Bend the pipe cleaners so that they lie on the wings.

You could use the bugs to decorate plant pots by pushing the stick into the soil.

The foil should be long enough to cover the stick.

7. Tape the pipe cleaners onto the bug's wings. You can then spread open the wings by bending the pipe cleaners.

8. Cut a strip of foil. Tape one end to the blunt end of a satay or kebab stick. Wind the foil along the stick, then tape the end.

9. Place the blunt end of the stick along the extra length of pipe cleaner. Wind the pipe cleaner tightly around the stick.

Bouncing bats

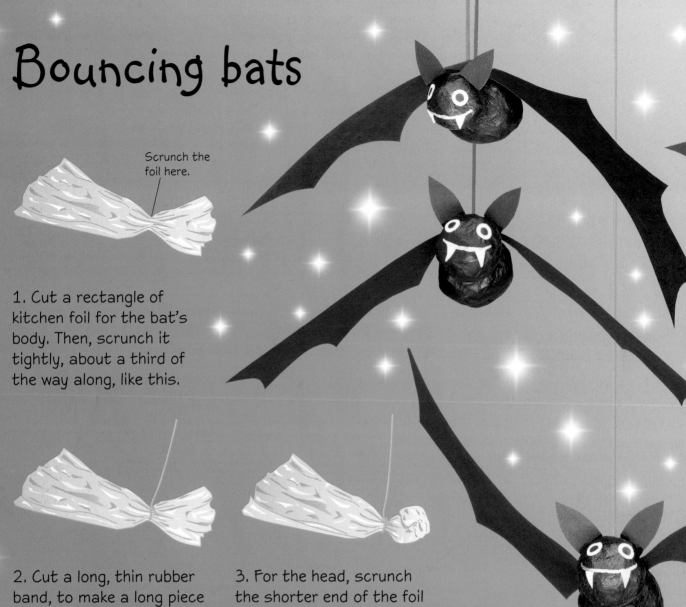

Scrunch the foil here.

1. Cut a rectangle of kitchen foil for the bat's body. Then, scrunch it tightly, about a third of the way along, like this.

2. Cut a long, thin rubber band, to make a long piece for hanging the bat. Tie one end tightly around the scrunched part of the foil.

3. For the head, scrunch the shorter end of the foil in on itself. As you scrunch the foil, bend it in to where the rubber band is tied.

Make sure that the rubber band still sticks out of the middle.

Pull the rubber band out to one side.

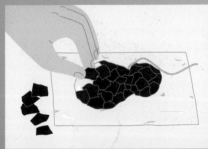

4. Scrunch the other end of the foil in the same way, to make the body. Then, squeeze the head and body, to make them rounded.

5. Rip lots of small pieces of black tissue paper. Then, lay the bat on plastic foodwrap and brush part of it with white glue.

6. Press pieces of tissue paper onto the wet glue. Then, brush on more glue and press on more paper, until the bat is covered.

Fold

Hold the layers together as you cut.

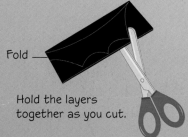

Fold the tabs up, like this.

Hang up the bat while the glue dries.

7. Fold a strip of black paper in half, with the short ends together. Draw a wing shape against the fold, then cut out the shape.

8. Draw two ears on black paper, with a tab at the bottom. Cut out the ears, then glue their tabs, and the wings, onto the bat.

9. Draw the bat's mouth with a silver pen. Then, draw eyes and fangs on white paper. Cut them out, then glue them on.

Party flags

These flags have been decorated with crowns and symbols copied from playing cards.

You could use bright thread or string to hang your flags on.

1. For a flag template, mark the middle points of each edge of a rectangle of cardboard. Join the dots, then cut out the shape.

2. Place the cardboard template on some bright crêpe paper and draw around it in pencil. Then, cut out the shape.

3. Make several flag shapes, in different shades of crêpe paper, in the same way. Then, fold them all in half, like this.

You can add sparkle to your flags by using shiny paper or putting glitter on them.

4. Cut out lots of small crowns, hearts, diamonds and fancy shapes. Glue the shapes to the fronts of the folded flags.

5. Cut out some even smaller shapes and glue them on top of the first ones. Then, unfold all the flags you have made.

6. Spread a flag with glue. Lay a piece of thread over the crease and fold the flag over it. Then, glue the rest of the flags onto the thread.

Hanging fish chains

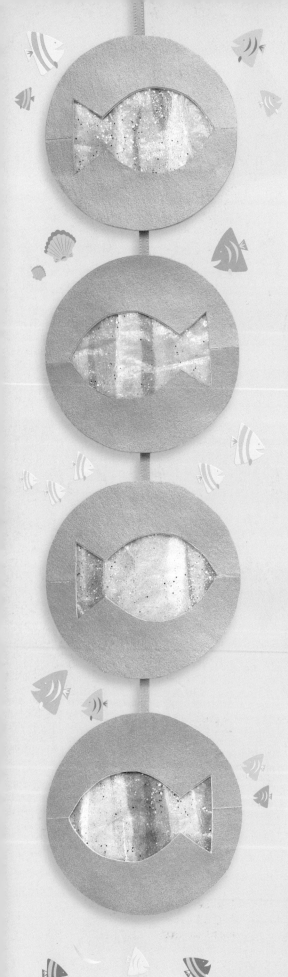

1. Rip different shades of tissue paper into thin strips. Then, lay a piece of white tissue paper on some plastic foodwrap.

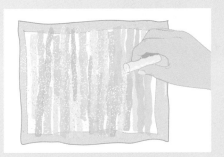

2. Brush white glue over the white tissue paper and press on the strips. Brush more glue over them, then sprinkle on a little glitter.

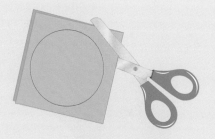

3. Fold a piece of paper in half. Place a mug on the paper and draw around it. Then, cut out the circle through both layers.

4. Holding the circles together, fold them in half. Draw the shape of half a fish against the fold, then cut it out.

5. Unfold both circles. Peel the striped tissue paper off the plastic foodwrap and glue one of the circles onto the tissue paper.

6. Repeat steps 3-5 three more times. Then, cut out all the circles that have been glued onto the tissue paper.

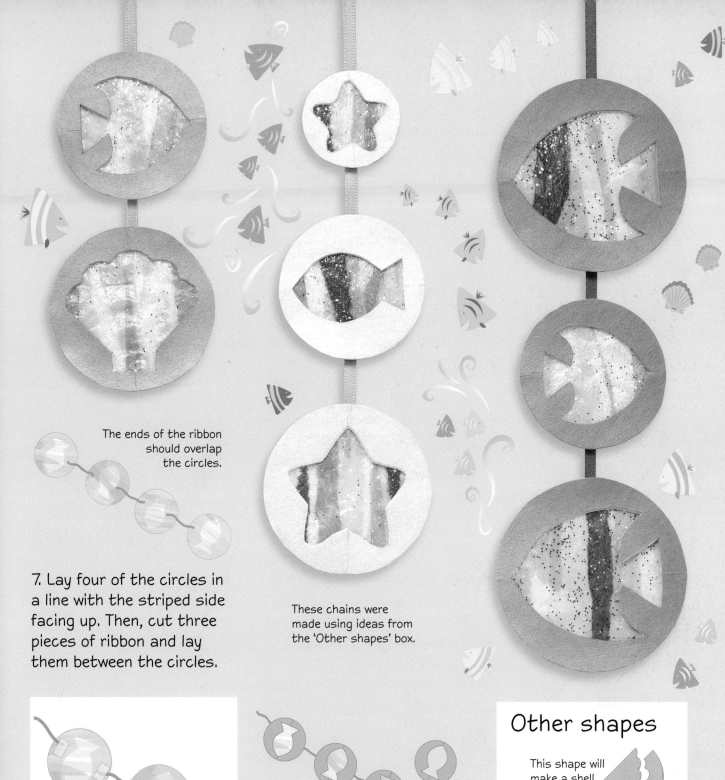

The ends of the ribbon
should overlap
the circles.

These chains were
made using ideas from
the 'Other shapes' box.

7. Lay four of the circles in
a line with the striped side
facing up. Then, cut three
pieces of ribbon and lay
them between the circles.

8. Tape the ribbon onto
the circles. Cut another
piece of ribbon for hanging
the chain and tape it onto
the top circle.

9. Glue the other circles
on top to hide the ribbon.
Glue them so that the
edges of the fish and
the circles line up.

Other shapes

This shape will
make a shell.

This shape will
make a starfish.

To make an angel
fish, cut out a
shape like this.

Pirate cutlass and hook

Cutlass

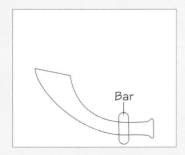

1. Draw a curved shape for the blade on a large piece of cardboard. Then, draw a handle with a bar across it, at one end of the blade.

Bar

2. Cut out the cutlass, then lay it back on the cardboard. Carefully draw around the cutlass, then cut out the shape.

The blades need to face each other.

3. Spread glue on one side of each blade. Press them onto a piece of kitchen foil, with the handles sticking off the edge, like this.

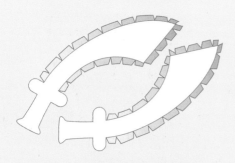

4. Cut around the blades, leaving a border. Then, make V-shaped cuts all around the border, to make the foil easier to bend.

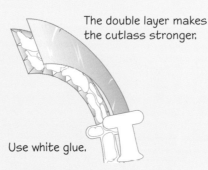

The double layer makes the cutlass stronger.

Use white glue.

5. Spread glue around the edge of each blade. Bend the foil over the edges and press it down. Then, glue them both together.

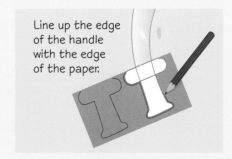

Line up the edge of the handle with the edge of the paper.

6. Lay the handle on some brown or gold paper. Draw around it, then turn it over and draw around it again. Then, cut out the shapes.

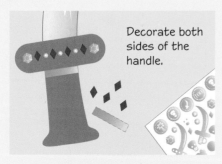

Decorate both sides of the handle.

7. Glue the paper shapes onto the handle. Then, decorate the handle with bright or shiny paper, foil, or stickers from this book.

You'll find jewel stickers in the middle of this book.

Hook

1. Draw around a large mug on a piece of cardboard. Then, draw curves for the blade. Add a handle with a bar across it.

2. Cut around the outline of the hook, then lay it back on the cardboard. Draw around it again, then cut it out.

3. Following steps 3-7 opposite, cover the blades with foil, then glue the hooks together. Glue paper onto the handles, too.

Draw watery swirls and leaf patterns.

4. Using a blunt pencil, draw patterns on the blade. Then, decorate the handle with bright or shiny paper, foil or stickers.

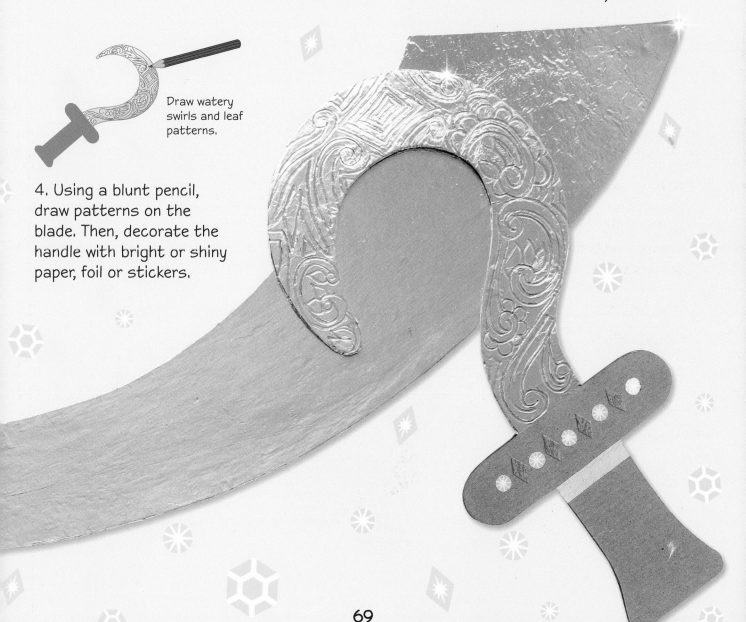

Cut-and-stick butterflies

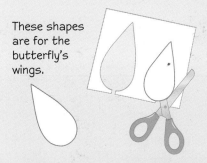

These shapes are for the butterfly's wings.

1. Draw two teardrops on a piece of thick cardboard. Make one a little smaller than the other. Then, cut out the shapes.

2. Lay the big teardrop on a piece of patterned paper or material. Draw around it, then draw around it again, to make two shapes.

3. Lay the small teardrop on a different piece of paper or material and draw around it twice. Then, cut out all four teardrop shapes.

4. Glue the big teardrops onto some thick paper, so that the pointed ends touch. Then, glue the small teardrops on below them.

5. Cut out a shape for the butterfly's body from some thick material. Then, glue the body down the middle of the wings.

6. Dip a thin paintbrush in some thick paint, then brush stripes across the body. Paint two dots for eyes, then add long feelers.

7. Cut out two circles from material and glue them onto the ends of the feelers. Then, glue a sequin on top of each circle.

8. Cut two more circles and glue them onto the wings. Draw stars on shiny paper and cut them out. Glue the stars onto the wings, too.

71

Decorated boxes

The boxes make perfect presents for birthdays or Mother's day.

Rub the shapes, to flatten them.

1. Cut lots of shapes from bright shades of paper. Then, brush them with white glue and press them all over a box.

2. Cut lots of pictures of different kinds of flowers from old magazines. Cut as close to the edges of the flowers as you can.

3. Brush some white glue onto the back of one of the paper flowers. Then, stick the flower onto the top of the box.

4. Gently rub the flower, to make it really flat. Then, glue another flower onto the box, a little way from the first one.

5. Glue on lots more flowers. Glue some of them so that they go over the edges of the box, then press them down.

6. Brush a thick layer of white glue over the whole box, including the flowers. Then, leave the glue to dry completely.

This was a round cheese box. It was painted and the flowers were stuck on when the paint was dry.

You could decorate the lid of a plain gift box.

For a yummy gift, fill a decorated box with chocolates.

Mermaid tiara

1. Cut a band of thin white cardboard that fits around your head. Cut a little off one end, as the tiara will sit on top of your head.

Glue the paper onto the tiara a little at a time.

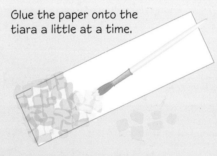

2. Rip lots of tissue paper into small pieces. Then, brush white glue over the band and press on the paper. Leave it to dry.

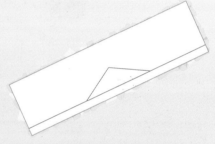

3. Turn the band over, then draw a line along it. Draw a wide triangle in the middle of the line with its tip halfway up the band.

4. Draw a curly wave on the tip of the triangle. Then, draw smaller waves down both sides of the triangle, like this.

Cut along the bottom, too.

5. Cut out the tiara around the waves. Then, pressing hard with a ballpoint pen, draw a curve down the middle of each wave.

6. Turn the tiara over. To make the waves 3-D, pinch along the lines you have drawn. Brush glue over the tiara and sprinkle glitter on.

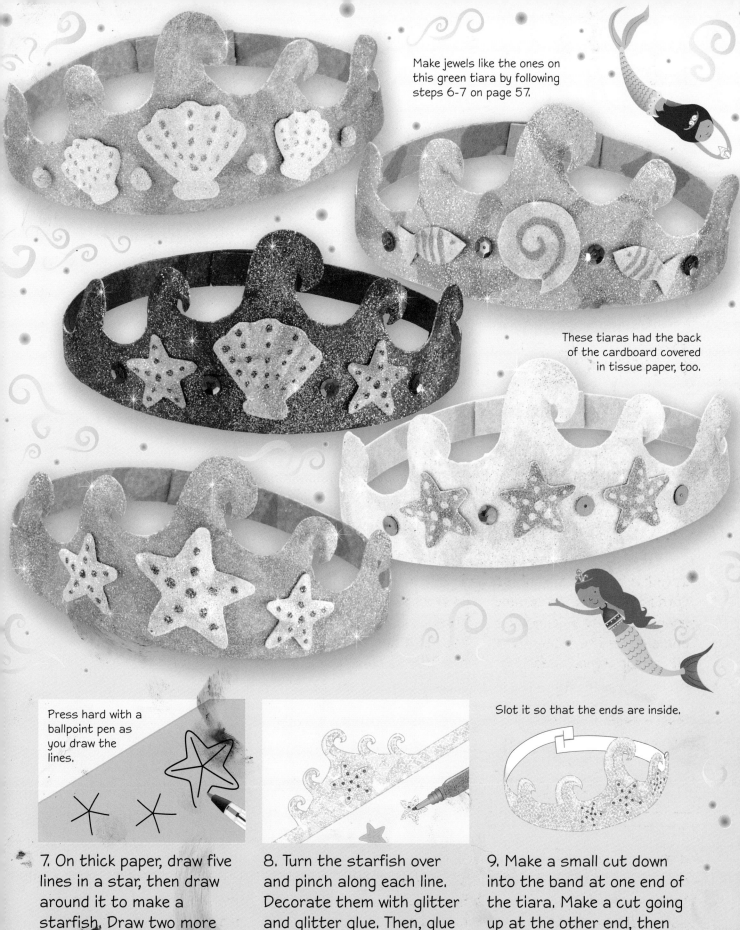

Make jewels like the ones on this green tiara by following steps 6-7 on page 57.

These tiaras had the back of the cardboard covered in tissue paper, too.

Press hard with a ballpoint pen as you draw the lines.

Slot it so that the ends are inside.

7. On thick paper, draw five lines in a star, then draw around it to make a starfish. Draw two more starfish and cut them out.

8. Turn the starfish over and pinch along each line. Decorate them with glitter and glitter glue. Then, glue the starfish onto the tiara.

9. Make a small cut down into the band at one end of the tiara. Make a cut going up at the other end, then slot the ends together.

Pirate paraphernalia
Telescope

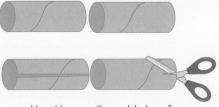

Use the cardboard tubes from inside rolls of paper towels.

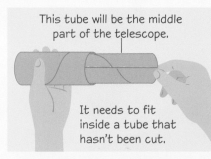

This tube will be the middle part of the telescope.

It needs to fit inside a tube that hasn't been cut.

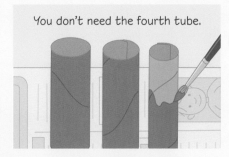

You don't need the fourth tube.

1. Very carefully, cut two cardboard tubes in half with a bread knife. Then, cut two pieces from end to end with scissors.

2. Spread glue next to the cut edge of one of the tubes. Overlap the two sides of the cut and hold them together tightly.

3. Glue the edge of the other cut tube. Overlap its edges, until it fits inside the middle part. When the glue is dry, paint the tubes.

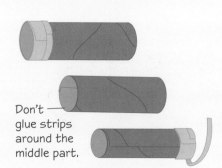

Don't glue strips around the middle part.

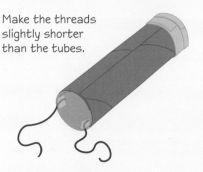

Make the threads slightly shorter than the tubes.

4. Cut a strip of cardboard. Glue it around the widest tube, then glue a thin strip on top. Then, do the same with the narrow tube.

5. To hold the three parts of the telescope together, cut four pieces of thread. Tape two of them inside the narrow tube, like this.

6. Slide the narrow tube inside the middle one. Tape the loose ends of the threads inside the end of the middle tube.

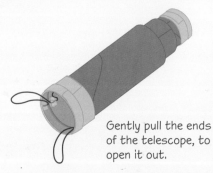

Gently pull the ends of the telescope, to open it out.

7. Tape the other two pieces of thread inside the middle tube. Slide it inside the widest one, then tape the ends of the threads.

This telescope was decorated with shiny stickers.

Shiny earring

1. Cut a piece of foil that is about the size of a postcard. Squeeze it in your fingers, then roll it on a flat surface, to make a thin stick.

The piece of foil secures the ends.

2. Bend the stick into a circle, then twist the ends together. Wrap a small piece of foil around the part where they join.

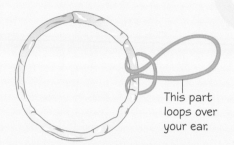

This part loops over your ear.

3. Lay the earring over a thin rubber band that will go around your ear. Then, push one end of the rubber band through the other.

Eye patch

Make the patch big enough to cover one of your eyes.

1. Draw an eye patch, then cut it out. Make a cut into it, then spread glue next to the cut. Overlap the edges and hold them together.

Tie the thread around your head.

2. Cut a piece of thread that will go around your head, plus some extra for tying it on. Tape it to the back of the eye patch.

You could glue cardboard shapes onto your telescope.

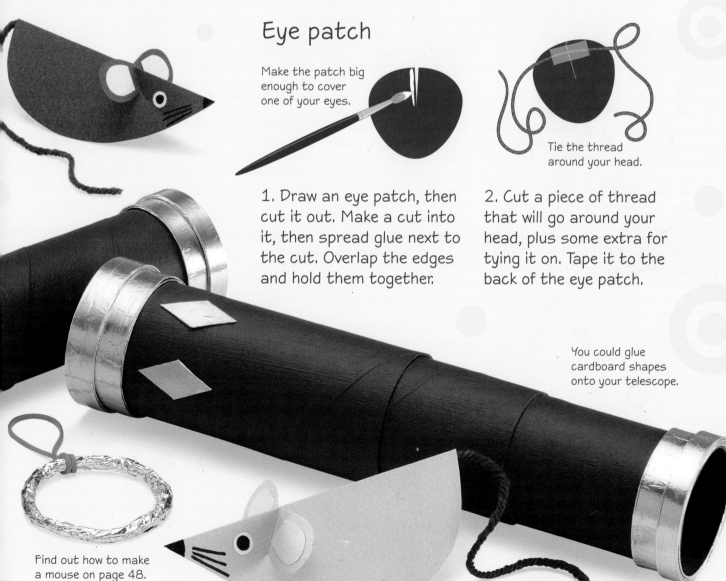

Find out how to make a mouse on page 48.

Printed collage card

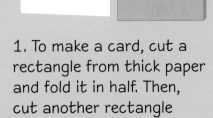

1. To make a card, cut a rectangle from thick paper and fold it in half. Then, cut another rectangle from thick cardboard.

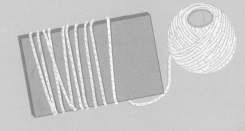

2. Tape the end of some string to the cardboard. Then, wind the string roughly around and around, like this.

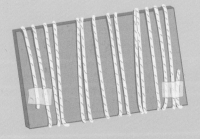

3. Wind the string all along the cardboard, then cut it. Tape the end on the same side of the cardboard as the other piece of tape.

4. Paint the string with yellow paint, so that it is covered. Then, press it onto the folded card, to print yellow lines.

5. Print more lines on the card, adding more paint as you go. Continue until the card is covered in lots of yellow lines, like this.

Try cutting out lots of small flowers.

You could add some paper leaves and a stalk.

6. Cut a square from yellow paper, smaller than the card. Then, cut an even smaller square from light green paper.

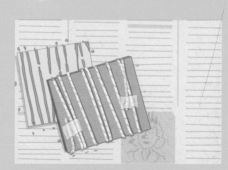

7. Wrap string around another piece of cardboard. Then, print green lines on the green square, as you did before.

8. Glue the yellow and green squares onto the card. Then, cut out a white paper flower and a yellow middle, and glue them on.

Zigzag Valentine card

Fold

1. To make the card, fold a long rectangle of thick paper, like this. The front part should be narrower than the back part.

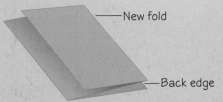

New fold

Back edge

2. Turn the paper over. Then, fold back the right-hand section, so that the new fold lines up with the back edge of the card.

You could decorate a tall card with a big heart and sequins.

Try adding extra sparkle with glitter glue.

Glue hearts along more than one edge of a card.

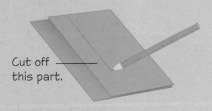

Cut off this part.

3. The front section should be about half of the width of the card. If it's wider, draw a pencil line down the card and cut along it.

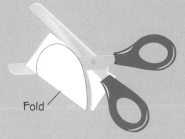

Fold

4. To make the heart decorations, fold a piece of thick paper in half. Draw half a heart against the fold, then cut it out.

5. Open out the heart. Lay it on a piece of pink paper and draw around it. Then, draw around it twice more on other pieces of paper.

You could decorate a card with a flower made from hearts.

The little heart in the middle was brushed with glue and sprinkled with glitter.

This card had different shades of paper glued inside and on the front.

Only glue the left side of each heart.

6. Cut out the hearts. Then, cut out another smaller heart from thick paper. Draw around it three times and cut out the shapes.

7. Glue one small heart onto each big heart. Then, glue the big hearts along the edge on the front of the card, like this.

8. Brush lots of dots of white glue around the edges of the hearts and press on sequins. Then, leave the glue to dry.

Easter egg card

1. To make patterned paper, dip a thick paintbrush into clean water. Then, brush the water all over a piece of thick white paper.

2. While the paper is still wet, blob different shades of bright watery paint on it. The paints will run into each other.

3. While the paint is drying, cut a rectangle from a piece of thick paper. Fold the paper in half to make a card.

4. Cut out four small squares, the same size, from white paper. Arrange them on the card and glue them on, like this.

5. Cut four more squares from tissue paper. Make them slightly smaller than the white squares. Glue them on top.

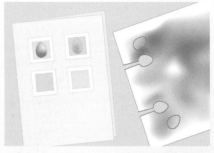

6. Cut out an egg from the patterned paper. Draw around it three times and cut out the eggs. Glue the eggs on top of the squares.

7. For a gift tag, cut an egg from the patterned paper. Punch a hole in the top with a hole puncher and thread some ribbon through.

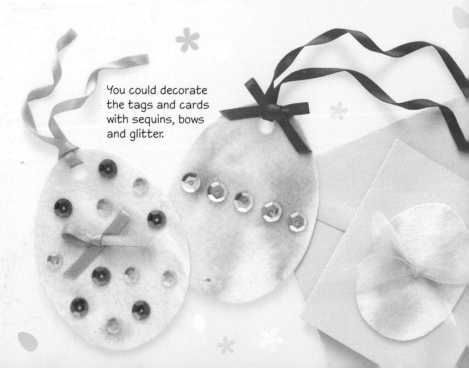

You could decorate the tags and cards with sequins, bows and glitter.

Use the ideas
shown here to
make lots of
different cards.

Painted butterflies card

The paint needs to be watery.

1. Pour some blue paint onto an old plate and mix it with water. Then, use a small brush to paint butterfly wings, like this.

2. Wash your brush. Then, while the blue paint is wet, dab small dots of green paint onto it. The green paint will spread a little.

3. Leave the paint to dry. Then, paint a dark blue body in the middle of the wings. Add thin feelers to the top of the body.

These cards are ideal for Mother's Day and birthdays.

4. Paint lots more butterflies. Try using orange and red paint together, and pink and yellow. Then, leave the paint to dry.

5. Make your painting into a card by folding a sheet of thick paper in half. Cut around the butterflies and glue them onto the card.

Leave a white border around the butterflies.

These butterflies have been splattered with paint (see below).

Splattering

Dip a dry brush into some runny paint. Then, pull a finger over the bristles, to splatter the paint over your picture.

Pop-up card

1. Cut two pieces of paper, so that they are the same size. Fold one of them in half, short edges together.

2. Make two cuts, the same length, in the middle of the folded edge. Fold over the flap between the cuts.

3. Turn the card over, fold the flap the other way and crease it. Unfold the flap, then open out the card.

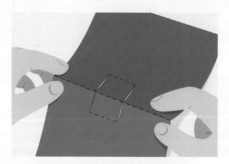

4. Pinch along the middle fold on either side of the flap. Hold it at each end of the fold, not near the flap.

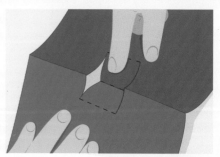

5. Push the flap down with your finger. Then, close the card carefully and smooth it flat. Open the card.

You could make one of these for a summer birthday card.

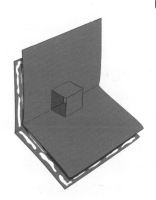

6. Fold the other piece of paper in half. Glue the two pieces together, like this, matching the middle folds.

7. Cut a piece of paper which is the same size as the card when it is folded. Draw a picture on it and cut it out.

8. Use felt-tip pens to decorate the inside of the card. Then, glue your picture onto the pop-up flap.

Halloween card

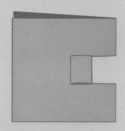

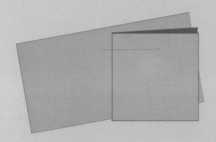 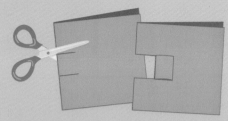

1. Cut two rectangles of thick paper 22x11cm (8½ x 4¼in.). Fold one of the rectangles in half, short sides together.

2. Make two cuts in the folded side, like this. Then, fold over the flap between the two cuts. Crease the fold well.

3. Turn the card over. Fold the flap again, creasing it well with your fingers. Then, unfold the flap and open the card.

You could use the cards for party invitations; write the date, time and place on the back.

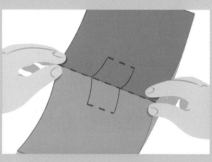

4. Pinch along the middle fold on either side of the flap. Do this at the ends of the fold, but not on the flap.

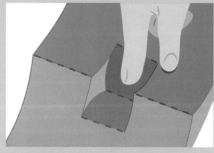

5. Push the flap down into the card, like this. Then, carefully close the card and smooth all the folds flat.

Don't get any glue on the flap.

Cut out a ghost from white paper at step 7 and glue it onto the box.

6. Open the card. The flap will pop up like a box. Fold the other rectangle in half. Glue it on to make a backing card.

You will draw the bat on the black paper.

Draw a witch's cat instead of a bat.

Glue on a paper moon or press on one of the stickers from the sticker pages.

7. To make sure that the bat won't show when the card is closed, cut a piece of paper which fits in the card, like this.

Cut a pumpkin from orange paper. Decorate it with felt-tip pens, then glue it on.

Press shiny star stickers on the background.

8. Draw a bat on the paper and cut it out. Put some glue on the front of the box and press the bat onto it.

Snowman card

Press star stickers in the sky around the snowman.

You could add stick arms with a felt-tip pen.

Cut a hat from black paper and glue it on.

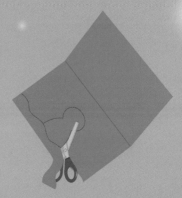

1. Cut a rectangle from blue paper. Then, cut a piece of thick white paper exactly the same size. Fold both of them in half.

2. Open the blue paper. Draw a wavy line across one side of the card for snow. Draw the outline of a snowman on the line.

3. Use scissors to cut along the line for the snow, then around the snowman and along the line for snow again.

4. Spread glue over the bottom half of the blue card. Then, press one side of the white card onto it, matching the edges.

5. Spread glue over the top of the blue card, around the snowman. Then, close the card, pressing it down onto the white card.

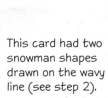

This card had two snowman shapes drawn on the wavy line (see step 2).

6. Draw eyes and a line of dots for the mouth. Add a nose and a hat and press on stickers for buttons.

Reindeer wrapping paper

1. Use a crayon to draw the body. Add a neck.

2. Draw the head and add two ears.

3. Add four long legs and a tail.

4. Crayon hooves, a nose and two eyes.

5. Draw jagged antlers on its head.

6. Add spikes to the antlers. Fill in with pens.

Make a long thin card.

Make a gift tag to match the paper.

To draw a fir tree

1. Draw the trunk of a tree with a crayon.

2. Add branches with a wax crayon.

3. Draw dark green branches over the top.

Draw lots of reindeer and trees on small pieces of paper. Then, glue them onto a large piece of bright wrapping paper.

Tie some ribbon around your present.

Printed papers

Jolly Roger paper

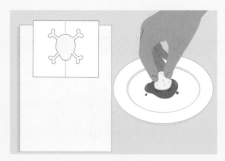

1. To make a stencil, fold a piece of thick paper in half. Draw half a skull and two bones against the fold, then cut along the lines.

2. Open out the stencil and lay it on a flat piece of paper. Spread some paint on an old plate, then dip a sponge into the paint.

3. Dab paint all over the hole, then lift off the stencil. When the paint is dry, draw eyes, a nose and a toothy grin on the skull.

You could decorate wrapping paper, gift tags and envelopes, too.

To Jolly Jake,

Ahoy there! I'm having a swashbuckling Pirate Party on Friday. Hope to see you there – don't forget your parrot...

From

Buccaneer Bob

Flower wrapping paper

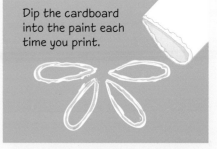
Dip the cardboard into the paint each time you print.

1. Cut a square of thick cardboard. Bend it around into a petal shape, then tape its edges together near the top.

2. Pour some paint onto an old plate and spread it out a little. Then, dip the bottom of the cardboard into the paint.

3. To print a flower, press the cardboard onto some paper, then lift it up. Print more petals. Then, print lots more flowers.

If you want to print a stalk, dip the edge of a piece of cardboard into some paint.

4. When the paint is dry, pour some yellow paint onto the plate. Fingerpaint middles for the flowers and let the paint dry.

Print the flowers on bright paper.

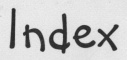

Index

accessories,
 make some fairy wings, 26-27
 mermaid necklace, 56-57
 mermaid shell purse, 42-43
 mermaid tiaras, 74-75
 party masks, 58-59

animals,
 bouncing bats, 62-63
 collage fish, 34-35
 cut-and-stick butterflies, 70-71
 dolphins to draw, 20-21
 hanging fish chains, 66-67
 make a glitter bug, 60-61
 make a mouse, 48
 octopus mobile, 54-55
 parrot painting, 6-7
 reindeer wrapping paper, 92-93
 sea horse pencil top, 49

cards,
 Easter egg, 82-83
 Halloween, 88-89
 painted butterflies, 84-85
 pop-up, 86-87
 printed collage, 78-79
 snowman, 90-91
 zigzag Valentine, 80-81
Christmas,
 make an advent calendar, 14-15
 reindeer wrapping paper, 92-93
 snowman card, 90-91
collage,
 cut-and-stick butterflies, 70-71
 cut-and-stick mermaids, 16-17
 fish, 34-35
 zigzag Valentine card, 80-81
cut-and-stick,
 butterflies, 70-71
 collage fish, 34-35
 mermaids, 16-17
 zigzag Valentine card, 80-81

decorations,
 bouncing bats, 62-63
 hanging fish chains, 66-67
 loveheart decoration, 46-47
 make some beads, 40-41
 octopus mobile, 54-55
 party flags, 64-65
 tissue paper chains, 32-33

drawing,
 dolphins to draw, 20-21
 farmyard scene, 22-23
 Halloween card, 88-89
 pirate treasure map, 4-5
 pop-up card, 86-87
 reindeer wrapping paper, 92-93
 snowman card, 90-91
 tractor picture, 10-11

Easter,
 decorated eggs, 30-31
 egg card, 82-83

fairy,
 make some fairy wings, 26-27
farm,
 farmyard scene, 22-23
 tractor picture, 10-11
flowers,
 decorated boxes, 72-73
 flower wrapping paper, 95
 loveheart decoration, 46-47
 painted plant pot, 52-53
 printed collage card, 78-79
 tissue paper chains, 32-33
 wax resist flowers, 8-9

Halloween,
 bouncing bats, 62-63
 card, 88-89
 carving pumpkins, 44-45

mermaid,
 cut-and-stick mermaids, 16-17
 handprinted mermaid, 24-25
 mermaids to paint, 12-13
 mirror, 38-39
 necklace, 56-57
 shell purse, 42-43
 tiaras, 74-75

painting,
 Easter egg card, 82-83
 handprinted mermaid, 24-25
 mermaids to paint, 12-13
 painted butterflies card, 84-85
 painted plant pot, 52-53
 parrot painting, 6-7
 pirate painting, 18-19
 printed collage card, 78-79

painting continued,
 printed papers, 94-95
 wax resist flowers, 8-9

pirate,
 cutlass and hook, 68-69
 finger puppet, 50-51
 Jolly Roger paper, 94
 make a treasure chest, 58-59
 painting, 18-19
 paraphernalia, 76-77
 treasure map, 4-5

things to make,
 bouncing bats, 62-63
 carving pumpkins, 44-45
 decorated boxes, 72-73
 decorated eggs, 30-31
 foil picture frame, 36-37
 hanging fish chains, 66-67
 loveheart decoration, 46-47
 make a glitter bug, 60-61
 make a mouse, 48
 make a treasure chest, 28-29
 make some beads, 40-41
 make some fairy wings, 26-27
 mermaid mirror, 38-39
 mermaid necklace, 56-57
 mermaid shell purse, 42-43
 mermaid tiaras, 74-75
 octopus mobile, 54-55
 party flags, 64-65
 party masks, 58-59
 pirate cutlass and hook, 68-69
 pirate finger puppet, 50-51
 pirate paraphernalia, 76-77
 sea horse pencil top, 49-50
 tissue paper chains, 32-33

Valentine,
 loveheart decoration, 46-47
 zigzag Valentine card, 80-81

wrapping paper
 printed papers, 94-95
 reindeer, 92-93